HERE COMES THE PIZZER

THE FOUND POETRY OF BASEBALL BROADCASTS

Edited by Eric Poulin

Foreword by Tim Wiles

Society for American Baseball Research, Inc.
Phoenix, AZ

Here Comes the Pizzer:
The Found Poetry of Baseball Broadcasts
Edited by Eric Poulin

Design: Gilly Rosenthol

All photographs in this book are provided by the
National Baseball Hall of Fame and Museum
Cover art: ROGER by Frank Cressotti

978-1-960819-34-5 (ebook)
978-1-960819-35-2 (paperback)
Library of Congress Control Number: 2025903202

Cronkite School at ASU
555 N. Central Ave. #406
Phoenix, AZ 85004
Phone: (602) 496-1460
Web: www.sabr.org
Facebook: Society for American Baseball Research
X: @SABR

HERE COMES THE PIZZER

THE FOUND POETRY OF BASEBALL BROADCASTS

For my mom, Judith Ann Poulin, Grand Marshall of the Easthampton Literacy Parade of the year 2000.

TABLE OF CONTENTS

WELCOME TO TODAY'S GAME

IN-GAME CHATTER

COMEDIES, OF ERRORS AND OTHERWISE

TRIUMPHS

TRAGEDIES

GOODBYE, FAREWELL, AND AMEN

FOREWORD: LOOK WHAT I FOUND!

BY TIM WILES

Thank you, Eric, and good afternoon everybody. I just hope these words arrive in time for publication. This is a dream come true, and I'm excited to have the opportunity to write an introduction to *Here Comes the Pizzer: The Found Poetry of Baseball Broadcasts.*

It is frequently noted that baseball is the sport most associated with literature, including poetry. So much of this game shines with meaning, and many great writers have successfully captured a bit of that essence in their work. New England poet Robert Francis, wrote what are—to this reader—the best six words ever written about baseball, in his poem "Pitcher": "Making the batter understand too late." Bart Giamatti wrote poetry in prose form in his essay "The Green Fields of the Mind." Ernest Lawrence Thayer mastered late-inning drama, hero worship, civic pride, and anticlimax in perhaps the nation's most familiar and beloved poem, "Casey at the Bat." Paul Simon asked us, so poignantly, "Where have you gone, Joe DiMaggio?" Franklin P. Adams gave us Tinker to Evers to Chance. If the Hall of Fame were to induct poets, it would include all those names, and many more: Walt Whitman, Robert Frost, Marianne Moore, Stephen Dunn, William Carlos Williams, May Swenson, Tom Clark, Quincy Troupe, Lawrence Ferlinghetti, Thomas Lux, Charles Bukowski, and Ogden Nash.

Poetry is like baseball in many ways. Perhaps the main way is that not everybody gets either of them. Many people give up on poetry or baseball because they claim not to understand them. Both poetry and baseball are often fabulously complex, and sometimes stunningly simple. Both take effort to understand and appreciate. Both are infinitely rewarding for those who make the effort. Both unfold before the viewer, and reward long-term attention and engagement.

Poetry has a long history that reaches back to ancient, even prehistoric times. There are hundreds of poetic forms, ranging from the extremely formal structures with rules of meter, rhythm, rhyme, syntax, and more, to the absolute freedom of free verse, freestyle, and improvisation.

One of the newer forms of poetry is *found poetry*. Some sources date this technique back a few hundred years, while others posit that it has developed because of all the words that are constantly before us, broadcast and published on the internet: speeches, song lyrics, magazine and newspaper articles, marketing and advertising copy, cereal boxes, pulp fiction—found poetry can be found anywhere where collections of words hang out. If you are prone to double meanings, and to thinking about how incoming language affects you, then you have likely stumbled upon some found poetry, even if you haven't written it down.

To use an example, or perhaps to offer a potentially entertaining writing prompt, consider MLB's standard broadcast disclaimer, which has been in use in one form or another since at least the mid-1970s, when I was an impressionable middle schooler: "This copyrighted telecast is the property of Major League Baseball, and pictures, descriptions, and accounts of this game may not be rebroadcast, retransmitted, or distributed without the expressed written consent of Major League Baseball." That's some language that many baseball fans hear every day. A practitioner of found poetry might enjoy turning it into a found poem by playing with the line breaks, combining this text with another familiar text, such as the Pledge of Allegiance, the Boy Scout oath, or even Shakespeare's 18th sonnet, which asks if he shall compare thee to a summer's day.

As it says on the internet, found poems start with existing text and play with that text to create something new, but also familiar, that adds a new meaning to that text, while also preserving the original meaning.

One of the poets included in this volume, Hart Seely, is a master of the found poetry form, a form which often chooses politicians, such as Sarah Palin, Donald Trump, George W. Bush, and Dick Cheney as its subjects, or perhaps, victims. Here is one of Seely's masterpieces, from his 2003 book *Pieces of Intelligence, The Existential Poetry of Donald H. Rumsfield.*

The Unknown

As we know,
There are known knowns.
There are things we know we know.
We also know
There are known unknowns.
That is to say
We know there are some things
We do not know.
But there are also unknown unknowns,
The ones we don't know
We don't know.

found by Rumsfeld at a Dept. of Defense briefing on 2/12/2002.)

What we have here are the actual words of Secretary Rumsfeld, arranged to emphasize the absurdity and complexity of espionage and warfare conducted by the government. If you don't see what Seely did here, or don't find it humorous and intriguing, the book you are holding may not be right for you.

As far as I know, Seely was the first poet to apply the found poetry concept to baseball broadcasts, who along with Tom Peyer, edited *O Holy Cow! The Selected Verse of Phil Rizzuto,* published in 2008, shortly after Rizzuto's death. The book was a revelation to Poulin, who told me that his "mind was blown by how the found poems alternated between absurd, hilarious, and incredibly poignant and quite touching. 'The Man in the Moon'—from that book—taken from the Yankees broadcast the night of Thurman Munson's funeral—was as perfect a piece of literature as you could find about dealing with grief while having to face the realities of the world." Poulin is right on that poem. With a nod to Casey Stengel, I suggest that "you could look it up." Just google it.

When long-time Red Sox player and broadcaster Jerry Remy passed away in 2021, Poulin reflected on the long presence, and sudden absence of Remy on the airwaves, and was inspired to propose this book to SABR's arts committee.

Poulin called for submissions from within SABR, and the results are wonderful. The various poems may lean toward the present day, but they are not presentist, in that they reach as far back as 1935, which is not too long after baseball broadcasting itself began to exist. While most broadcasts drifted up into the ether and disappeared forever, a few were archived for posterity. Well, we are posterity, and thanks to this technique, we can travel back in time to Game Four of the 1935 World Series pregame show, narrated by Boake Carter. If there are any research purists who are taken aback by SABR publishing a book of poetry, consider that until I read this manuscript, I thought I knew, from multiple sources, that Wrigley Field was the first ballpark to have a public address system, installed in 1941. Wrigley may well have been first, but this found poem pushes the installation date back to at least 1935:

The music today was supplied in its initial stage
by the Wrigley Field loudspeaker system.

> And it is a good system
> because it can be heard perfectly all
> over the field
> from the horns lodged in the big green
> scoreboard
> in back of deep center.

A formerly ephemeral source can now be considered a primary source.

Poulin and his contributors, as well as Cecilia Tan, SABR editor extraordinaire, have produced an excellent volume of found poetry. A diverse array of broadcasters and years are featured, from Red Barber to Harry Caray to Snoop Dogg. We visit Disco Demolition Night, an AAGPBL game, and the birth of Tommy John surgery. In chatting with Eric, I expressed my opinion that I wished this fine book were a little longer. He agreed, and hopes that this initial effort will be followed up with at least another volume with wider participation, once the techniques of searching for, finding, and shaping found poetry are disseminated to SABR members via this volume, as Steve Stone would say. (If you are a longtime Stone listener, you'll know how often he says something like "Sandberg reaches first base via the walk.")

In fact, you could watch old Cubs and White Sox games, and come up with a fun list of Steve Stone vias, which could be a silly found poem.

ACKNOWLEDGEMENTS

First and foremost, my incredible love and thanks go to my wife Gaby, who puts up with all of my wacky schemes and ideas. A lifetime of gratitude goes to Rick Teller, who introduced me to Hart Seely and Tom Peyer's brilliant work of Phil Rizzuto's found poetry; if you ever think the words and wisdom of a librarian can't change your life—guess again. Claudette Scrafford and Cassidy Lent at the National Baseball Hall of Fame and Museum were incredibly generous with their time and energy. Bruce McClure of the Clyde Sukeforth Chapter of SABR has been this project's top cheerleader and is tireless in his advocacy for baseball research and storytelling. Tim Wiles continues to be both an amazing mentor and better friend. Frank Cressotti's art breathes color and life into the game in a unique and fascinating way. Cecilia Tan fielded every tiny little question I had with the smoothness of Nomar in the late '90s. Finally, my biggest possible sky point to perhaps the last person on Earth I expected to become my literary muse—the late, great Gerald Peter Remy.

WELCOME TO TODAY'S GAME

THANK YOU, DON
FOUND BY ERIC POULIN

Thank you, Don—
And good evening, everyone.
And I just hope the words arrive in time for the opening pitch.

I suppose there are many fans listening right now,
Who held a lifetime ambition to be a major league baseball player.

I was one of them.

Don was one.

And Don has been with baseball—Major League Baseball
For twenty years.

And tonight I'm a thirty four year old rookie,
And I have to be the most excited man in the ballpark.

This is a dream come true.

And I'm excited to have the opportunity,
Provided by Gene Autry.

Dick Enberg
April 8, 1969
Pilots at Angels (First game of Dick Enberg's
51-year career)
Pregame Show

LIVESTOCK REPORT
FOUND BY KURT BLUMENAU

Here at the Oakland Coliseum
as we look out onto the field
we see the A's famous mule mascot,
Charlie O.
He's got a couple little kids on him out there
and doing a fine job.

Incidentally,
tomorrow night,
we have a pleasant surprise for the fans
who will be coming for our Family Night game.
Stan Cosca,
who's the trainer for Charlie O the mule,
is going to have Cricket.
Now that's the world's smallest registered horse.

He'll be on the field here with Charlie O
a half hour before game time
through the courtesy of Mr. and Mrs. Ray Ely,
who have brought Cricket
to the Oakland Coliseum
for many farmer's days in the past
and various other occasions.

He's really a cute little pony –
The world's smallest!
And he'll be out here
with one of the world's most honored mules,
Charlie O,

who's been having a little lumbago in his back,
they tell us lately,
but he's up and at 'em
here again today
and feels very good about
getting out there.

Monte Moore
August 11, 1974
Boston at Oakland
Pregame Show

I WANNA TELL 'YA

FOUND BY ERIC POULIN

between the fireworks the music
the disco music the burning of the thing
you know you're lucky you don't go nuts here

you know I've been there

I wanna tell 'ya
there's a big chance of going nuts
how can you even read the lineup when you can't even think

right now there's 30,000 kids
they got dirty signs all over this park

I wanna tell 'ya
unbelievable

a guy like me
who never thinks
like anything
like they are putting out here

this is unbelievable

I wanna tell 'ya—

But let's get back to the lineup.
Whittaker will bat second and play at second base.

Jimmy Piersall
July 12, 1979 (Disco Demolition Night)
Tigers at White Sox
Pregame Show
First game of scheduled doubleheader.

DANCE OF THE GROUNDSKEEPER
FOUND BY HART SEELY

The music today was supplied in its initial stage
by the Wrigley Field loudspeaker system.
And it is a good system.
because it can be heard perfectly all over the field
from the horns lodged in the big green scoreboard
in back of deep center.
Snappy tunes and records were played.
And in the midst of it all,
the catchy, foot-warming tune of Tiger Rag
blared out over the field.
And on the field at that time
were the groundsmen with the hose,
watering the cinder paths and laying the dust.
And the pressure of the water
sent a stream from the nozzle
spraying in fine, misty sheets
of some 75 or a hundred feet.
And the streams of Tiger Rag
suddenly tickled the fancy of the hoseman.
And so with nonchalant abandon,
he began to perform a high-class clog-down,
jiggling the hose in his flying spray
in time with the music,
for which performance he received a round laugh
and a burst of applause from the bleacherites.
Quite a wag was this fellow.
For having finished the watering of the bases,
He doubled out with three base bags,
skipping between second and first base,
with the little fancy trips that ballroom dancers give,
meanwhile strumming the first base sack

as though it were a mandolin.

It's too bad the Broadway producers weren't in their boxes

Boake Carter

October 5, 1935 (Game Four of the World Series)

Tigers at Cubs

Pregame Show

HAD TO MAKE A DECISION
FOUND BY RAY NIELSEN

Should the Oakland A's win the world championship again in 1974,
It could be because of the elbow
you're looking at right now.
It belongs to Tommy John,
Who at the all-star break was the winningest pitcher in the
National League.

Tommy,
you had a thirteen-and-three record.
You never picked up another victory after that.
Right Tony,
I tried to pitch.
I think I waited about eight or nine weeks and rested some.
…Tried to come back and throw.

It just got to the point to where… I could throw maybe three-quar-
ter's speed,
But whenever I tried to get the little extra pop of the ball…
I just couldn't do it.

And I couldn't throw a good curve ball.
I think I'd have to have both of them to win.

…The season was growing short.

I had to make a decision,
to get my arm operated on,
or try to maybe play in the series.

I felt the longer I waited, the more it would take me into spring
training.

So, we decided about the first of September to get my arm
operated on.

On the twenty-fifth, Dr. Frank Jobe went in and reconstructed my
left elbow.
And I like to think...I can come back next year and play next year.

Tommy John, I hope you do come back,
Because you're an important factor for the National League
And this ball club, the Dodgers.

I'm sure I will Tony.

Tony Kubek and Tommy John
October 16, 1974
Athletics at Dodgers—Game 4 of the 1974 World Series
Pregame Show

WAITING SINCE 1918
FOUND BY KURT BLUMENAU

Eddie Popowski the acting manager today;
also, today is his birthday.
And another birthday we'll mention in just a moment …

Here is the pitch and it's in the dirt.

Dennis B. Tremblay
of St Johnsbury Center, Vermont:
Ninety-six years old today.

Avid Red Sox fan
And listens to, follows the Red Sox on radio

Happy birthday,
Mr. Tremblay.

There's a swinging strike dropped by the catcher Herrmann.
Aparicio goes to first but the throw beats him.
And that's two away.

…

Hit on the ground on one hop to short,
picked up by Luis Alvarado,
throws to first in time.

An easy one-two-three inning for Wilbur Wood.

Red Sox out in order.

Ned Martin
August 20, 1927
Boston Red Sox at Chicago White Sox
Wilbur Wood pitching to Luis Aparicio
Top of the first, two out
Scoreless game.

IN-GAME CHATTER

THE MOON IN JUNE
FOUND BY ERIC POULIN

Now, Hebner's usually a fun-loving guy—
I don't know why he would be so irate.
Maybe he's got an early date?
(Or something)
And the game is running late!

Harry Caray
June 20, 1980
Tigers at White Sox
Steve Trout pitching to Lou Whittaker
Top of the 11ᵗʰ, one out
Detroit leading 4-3

YOU'D BE AMAZED
FOUND BY ERIC POULIN

It's one of those nights,
Where you don't need the windshield wipers going all the time.
It's like that hesitation—
The delayed windshield wiper.

You ever get mad at the delay?
Like you want it to go more?
You should get it checked.

Or try the adjustment—
The little adjustment on the side?
If you go and just spin a little dial on the side
You can adjust your delay.

When you get in your car tonight, check that out—
You'd be amazed with what cars have these days.

Jerry Remy
June 27, 2013
Blue Jays at Red Sox
Jon Lester pitching to Edwin Encarnacion
Top of the 6th, two out.
Boston leading, 7-2.

WHAT I TOLD YOU
FOUND BY ERIC POULIN

Sanchez on the one-two—
Unnhhh!!!

What I told you,
Get it in there,
Oh he in there!

That's Sanchez!
That's GS
What I told you, baby!

You call that an easy walk in the park—that's a base hit.

Give him a single,
He does like to mingle,
And my favorite jingle
Is the S to the N to the Double-O-No-No.

Snoop Dogg
June 15, 2024
Reds at Brewers
Andrew Abbott pitching to Gary Sanchez
Bottom of the 2nd, nobody out
Scoreless game

HOWARD IN THE DOGHOUSE
FOUND BY MARK STERNMAN

Understand there's a big doghouse
out in the bullpen
with Elston Howard's name on it.

I think he'd be
a little upset and insulted
if he didn't make it out there
some time during the season.

Although I will say this:
It's hard for me to understand
how Elston Howard
can get in anybody's doghouse.

Jerry Coleman
September 27, 1968
Yankees at Red Sox
Fred Talbot pitching to Russ Gibson
Bottom of the 4th, 2 on, nobody out
Boston leading, 4-1

TIMES HAVE CHANGED
FOUND BY ERIC POULIN

Infield In
One out
Morrison the batter
Game tied 1-1

There's a base hit!
Left field
White Sox lead 2-1

With the infield in
Boy oh boy

How times have changed!

Can you imagine the great Yankee team
Playing in
In the second inning?????????

They gotta be turning over in their graves!

Harry Caray
June 11, 1981
Yankees at White Sox
Bottom of the second, runner at third, one out
Game tied 1-1

LET'S BE HONEST ABOUT IT
FOUND BY ERIC POULIN

You know what's amazing about those tours
Is how many people come up and say

Wow!

What a great view this is!
And it is—it really is.
But they're—like—stunned about how nice it is

Up here.

But let's be honest about it.
We're missing a couple of chairs up top.

And a TV.

Jerry Remy
June 6, 2015
Athletics at Red Sox
Jesse Chavez pitching to Alejandro De Aza
Bottom of the 4th, one out
Boston leading, 4-1.

AN ETERNAL TRUTH
FOUND BY KURT BLUMENAU

The Cubs

Can ill afford to lose

Any game at all.

Byrum Saam
September 23, 1973
Chicago at Philadelphia
Rick Reuschel pitching to Willie Montanez
Bottom of the first, two out, runner on first base.
Phillies leading, 4-1

NOT ALL HEROES WEAR CAPES
FOUND BY ERIC POULIN

I would like to disappear.
Like that.
Forever.
Anytime you're in a situation,
You know—
Where you want to get away,
Just to be able to snap your fingers—
And disappear.

And reappear.

Like—for example—
Flying to the West Coast.
Wouldn't it be nice to go,
Poof?
Right in Seattle.
You're right there,
No problems.

I don't know if that's a superhero that does things like that.
But—I mean,
I would like to be able to do that.

Jerry Remy
July 31, 2012
Tigers at Red Sox
Rain Delay
Boston ahead, 4-1

CATCHING THE BEES
FOUND BY KURT BLUMENAU

The tall left-hander is ready.
Here's the payoff pitch to Ellis:

It's hit on the fists, foul, on the right side.

That really hurt!
Ellis came out of the batter's box,
threw the bat down
and shook both hands.

It's an expression they use in baseball,
Is: "You just caught the bees."

In other words, that bat rings in your hands.
And it's like somebody giving you
a little electric shock or something.

It burns sometimes, it hurts so much.

Jerry Coleman
July 13, 1969 (Game Two of doubleheader)
Yankees at Senators
Jim Shellenback pitching to John Ellis
Bottom of the 4th, two out, Runners on 2nd and 3rd, Full Count
Washington leading, 3-0

OK COMPUTER
FOUND BY ERIC POULIN

Nolan Ryan's allowed one hit
In the first three innings
And he has struck out five

And they're saying nasty things
About Nolan Ryan
That he doctors the baseball.

Yup.

Oh really?
What inning are we in now?

This is it, folks—The Computer says!!!

Jack Buck
May 22, 1987
Cardinals at Astros
Nolan Ryan pitching to Ozzie Smith
Top of the 4th, nobody out
Houston leading, 1-0

THREE VIEWS OF A SCORCHER (I)
FOUND BY KURT BLUMENAU

Well, the sun's come out again,
and it means it'll get even hotter
Here in Chicago now.

The only redeeming feature of this entire city is that it's windy.

On a hot summer day
you usually get quite a wind
in off the lake,
And we've been getting it so far today,
And that's the only thing that's kept the town
and particularly the press section
here at Comiskey Park
from feeling like a bake oven.

We'll run into these good hot days.

By George, we like it better than that snow
that covers the fields and the ground
During the wintertime.

Al Hefler
July 1, 1953
St. Louis Browns at Chicago White Sox
Bottom of the 3rd, nobody out, nobody on
Browns leading, 2-1

THREE VIEWS OF A SCORCHER (II)
FOUND BY KURT BLUMENAU

The tempo of this ballgame
will probably slow down considerably
as the afternoon wears on

Because it's hot
Out on that diamond.

To say that these guys
were perspiring profusely
would be an understatement.

Man, they're drenched already.

Al Hefler
July 1, 1953
St. Louis Browns at Chicago White Sox
Dick Littlefield pitching to Ferris Fain
Bottom of the 3rd, two on, nobody out
Browns leading, 2-1

THREE VIEWS OF A SCORCHER (III)
FOUND BY KURT BLUMENAU

Well, as I said, Art,
The complexion has changed, old buddy.

Yes, Al, I think
that wind's changed a little bit too
I can get a slight whiff
Of the stockyards.

Whaddya mean a slight whiff
of the stockyards, brother?
That's a full blast!

They must be doing business over there!

I got news for ya: It's a bumper crop!

Yeaaaaah …

… yeah, Chicago's a great town, Art.

The more you're in it,
the more you know about it,
One way or another.

Al Hefler and Art Gleeson
July 1, 1953
St. Louis Browns at Chicago White Sox
Dick Littlefield pitching to Ferris Fain
Bottom of the 3rd, two on, nobody out
Browns leading, 2-1

BETTER THAN LONG PANTS
FOUND BY ERIC POULIN

Dottie Schroeder is quite confident that
Her hair won't get in her eyes
And keeping her eye on the ball
Is catcher Kate Vonderau.
Okay, gals—play ball!

Pat Scott *has quite a curve*
But this one is wide
And Jean Marlowe is willing to wait.

Jean bunts it—**the squeeze is on!**
Tiby Eisen slides home with the run
And a nicely bruised leg.
Better a bruise than long pants—

EH, GALS????????

1951 Newsreel footage
Fort Wayne Daisies and Racine Belles (preseason training)
National Archives
Washington, DC

44

DIVINE MANDATE FOR BEARDS
FOUND BY GABRIEL BOGART

I'm not gonna do it now
cuz there's two outs
and the bases empty

looking at these players
with these big beards…
I decided to do some research, on beards

two down, second inning, no score
first pitch fastball for a strike

back to the dawn of humanity
beards evolved, number one, because
ladies liked them
and number two, because
it was the idea of
frightening off adversaries and wild animals

here's the one strike pitch
swung on and missed, strike two

it was so serious, if you look it up
there was a divine mandate
in Leviticus and Deuteronomy

Stripling…strike two pitch to Norris
which is promptly hit
into right field in front of Kiké

Vin Scully
April 30, 2016
Padres at Dodgers
Ross Stripling pitching to Derek Norris
Top of the 2nd, two out.
Scoreless game.

WHY DOES THIS SAUCE TASTE SANDY?
FOUND BY HARRISON GOLDEN

Charlie Dressen had a recipe
For a crab sauce he used to make
In the clubhouse
In the office
For the guys that were his pals,
But never for the players.

Al Spangler and I used to take sand
Out of the sandboxes in the clubhouse,
Where they would put out cigarettes.
We used to throw some of that in the crab sauce
Then watch everybody eat.
It was really kind of neat.

I tried it myself.
I remember that
Like it was,
Well, a long time ago.

Bob Uecker
July 11, 2014
Cardinals at Brewers
Yovani Gallardo pitching to Jon Jay
Top of the 4th, 2 out, nobody on.
Milwaukee leading, 6-2

MISTER BROADCASTER
FOUND BY CECILIA TAN

He gave me the best bit of advice
Ever
When I was just starting on the radio
and I'd been doing stuff on TV as pre- and post-game host.

He sat down next to me
before an Old Timers Game
on the Yankee bench. He said:
Can I give you a little bit of advice.

Me
being arrogant
I said of course not—
Just kidding—I said Of Course Sir.

And he said: when you're on TV
It sounds like you're talking to me
But when you get on the radio, you become
Mister Broadcaster.

You're trying to talk to millions of people
And then you're not talking to anybody.
So let me ask you—
is there somebody you know is listening.

I said, yeah, my mom is always listening.
He said, okay, here's what you should do—
Broadcast to your mom. Just talk to her.

If you just talk to your mom,
then everybody that's listening to the radio
is going to think that you're talking just to them.

Michael Kay (speaking about Mel Allen)
August 22, 2023
Nationals at Yankees
Pregame Show

SHOVELING PARTLY CLOUDY
FOUND BY HART SEELY

There was a mystery,
It was a Perry Mason mystery,
And the people involved
Were a television news thing.
And the guy called out,
Out to the weather guy,
(They were off the air at the time,)
"By the way, Gary,
"I've had to shovel
"A lot of 'Partly Cloudy' lately!"
Here's the oh-one to Crawford.
Swung on, lined to left...

John Sterling
April 4, 2008
Rays at Yankees
LaTroy Hawkins pitching to Carl Crawford
Top of the 8th, two out
Tampa Bay leading, 10-4

BING DOES THE STADIUM
FOUND BY JIM ARMENTI

Here's the next pitch to Johnny Pesky
Strike! Called! One and one.
Johnny Pesky. Very fine ball player
Johnny good type of athlete high class
clean living fella, very popular with his
players and with the fans alike.
(he's a) left handed hitter has sort of a half open stance
at the plate.
Here's the next pitch to **him...**
He hits a line smash
which is taken by the first baseman
and doubles uh Dominic DiMaggio off second
no play at first base that's the second out.
First baseman Souchock took that smash
on the first hop and uh threw out Dominic DiMaggio
by a step. DiMaggio was flying down the
    baseline but couldn't make it.
Now we got the mighty uh heh, Ted Williams up there.

Bing Crosby
April 23, 1948
Red Sox at Yankees
Joe Page pitching to Johnny Pesky
Top of the 6th, one out
Boston leading, 4-0

CRO AND THE RAVEN
FOUND BY TIM WILES

With one out in a 6-6 ballgame, here's Bobby, back from the woods.
Back from where?
The latrine.
You really are a man utterly lacking in tact.
It's my military training

This'll be a long throw for Dunston, and he gets Nettles.
There is no long throw for Shawon Dunston. He can throw guys out
from deep left field with that arm.

He has learned to control it.

He has learned to throw it as hard as he has to. On ground balls like
this, he has learned to adjust his footwork. Ruben Amaro helped him
with that. John Vuckovich helped him, and Stick, the former short-
stop Gene Michael, has really stabilized Shawon Dunston.

This has truly been a long day's journey into a dark, dark night for
Ozzie Virgil, O for six, five strikeouts, ball one.
You're starting to sound like Edgar Allen Poe in this extra inning
ballgame. Quoth the raven, we'll hear that next.
Nevermore..........
The record for strikeouts in a game is six. A game of any length, extra
inning or regulation. If Virgil comes up empty in this turn, he's tied
that mark. But, Moyer's behind him, 3-0.
Moyer just aimed that last pitch, 2-0, said here it is, hit it, but he
couldn't find the strike zone. Didn't have a whole lot on it........

Takes a rip, and bounces it foul. Well, you going to St. Louis or back to New York and see Randy and Keith? You may miss a few planes. I've got a short trip, to Wisconsin, couple hundred miles. It's fun, isn't it?

Hey!

I mean not that it's fun missing your plane, I mean it's fun being at Wrigley. We're gonna get a chance to hear Harry, I believe, as he walks, in the 14th! Harry's getting the voice in tune. They've been chanting for him for two innings.

No matter what happens, it beats having a real job, I'll tell you that. Alright, here comes Thomas. Top half of the 14th, tied at six.
Are we gonna have a pinch runner now? I saw some movement in the dugout for Chuck Tanner. Apparently not. O for six. Fastball outside. Tanner just thought to get the bullpen going again.
In comes Trillo, he makes a nice play on a short hop, and he throws Thomas out. Boy, talk about wearing a big league collar, Thomas is o for seven. To the last of the 14th.

Here comes Harry!
Since this is the second seventh inning stretch, it's time for Harry to reprise his number here.
Hey, my former third base coach, Frankie Crosetti, who was in this ballpark the day that Babe Ruth allegedly called his shot—the Cubs team being swept in four games in the World Series— would have said 'What is this game coming to, a broadcaster singing Take Me Out to the Ball Game. Ah but if The Crow was here, he's out in the San Francisco Bay area, he'd've loved Harry too.

He's a beauty, isn't he?

What is this game coming to? That kind of stuff is what this game should always be about!

Bob Costas and Tony Kubek
May 23, 1987
Braves at Cubs
Jamie Moyer pitching to Ozzie Virgil
Top of the 14th, one out
Game tied, 6-6

COMEDIES,
OF ERRORS
AND OTHERWISE

TOMORROW'S AN OFF DAY
FOUND BY ERIC POULIN

This is a first.
I've never lost a tooth.
I've really lost a tooth!

NO!

You can't see it?
There it is—the tooth.
I think it's a cap.
I think it's a cap is what it is.
It's got a nail in it.

There it is.

It just fell right out.
I'm not going to put it back in.
I don't think you can do that—I'm not going to try it.

I'm not a dentist.
Tomorrow's an off day, I'd rather get this thing taken care of.

Jerry Remy
July 2, 2014
Cubs at Red Sox
Brandon Workman pitching to Mike Olt
Top of the 4th, one out.
Chicago leading, 3-1

SOMETHING FUNNY
FOUND BY ERIC POULIN

Can I ask you a question, Don?
When I say Xander Bogaerts, is there something funny about that,
The way I say it?

Okay—I'm just curious.

Well, yesterday, when we were coming home from the game,
And we were on a bus that had a lot of fans
That stay at the same hotel we are.
And I had a nice lady behind me tap me on the shoulder.

And she said,
Hey can you say Xander Bogaerts for my son?
So—I said

Sure.

So I said Xander Bogaerts,
And they all started laughing.

Jerry Remy
June 28, 2015
Red Sox at Rays
Chris Archer pitching to Xander Bogaerts
Top of the 4th, one out
Boston ahead, 2-0

I COULDA BEEN A CONTENDER
FOUND BY ERIC POULIN

Awww—he's telling her how he used to do it!

Yeah—I remember when I was in high school—I threw that nasty
curveball.
You should have seen him!
It had a big rotation on it.
Yeah—I'll show you pictures when we get back home.
I've got some video too—
It's black and white but it's going to be great,
You know what I mean?

She's not buying it, either!
It's like—no.
Please stop talking.

Oh really?
Yeah—I mean, I was great
You should have seen it
I could have gone pro
But I had an argument with a coach
And we didn't quite see eye to eye.

Yeah.

And that trick elbow got me.
And he didn't like that I wore my hat backwards.

Brian Anderson
August 18, 2021
Milwaukee at St. Louis

THREE-TWO, GOOD BUDDY
FOUND BY ERIC POULIN

Three-two.

Swung on—
A pop foul back here.

OWWW!!!

OW!!!

OWWW!!!!!!

It really hit me.
I didn't know it was coming back that far!

So, once again, it will be a three-two.

—John Sterling
June 10, 2023
Red Sox at Yankees
Clay Holmes pitching to Justin Turner
Top of the 9th, two out
New York leading, 3-1

HERE COMES THE PIZZER

FOUND BY ERIC POULIN

Now, Don.
Between innings we did some investigative reporting,
On who and what was thrown at that gentleman.
And that gentleman has been ejected,
But it was an ugly, ugly sight.
And I don't know why it was necessary.

Now.

Watch.

I can't circle because I don't have my telestrator
But here comes the pizzer—now see it?
Oh, jeez!
The guy with the Patriots jacket
And of course he's been asked to leave the ballgame
For ruining a good piece of pizzer.

Jerry Remy
April 16, 2007
Angels at Red Sox
JC Romero pitching to Orlando Cabrera
Top of the 8th, nobody out
Boston leading, 7-1.

GOD REST YE, MERRY GENTLEMEN (I)
FOUND BY ERIC POULIN

Are you one of those guys
That goes crazy
Like, decorating The House around Christmastime?

My wife does a very nice job
Decorating The House.

I enjoy looking at everything.
We keep it up 'til New Years.

Jerry Remy
September 28, 2012
Orioles at Red Sox
Top of the seventh, one out.
Jon Lester pitching to Nate Mclouth.
Baltimore ahead, 4-2

GOD REST YE, MERRY GENTLEMEN (II)
FOUND BY ERIC POULIN

I'll tell you one thing I would never do,
Is have a Christmas party,
Because you can't get rid of the people.

You know what I mean?

You see these houses—
With cars lined up all the way down the road.

And all I can think of is:
When is the last person going to leave this party?
Because you know he is dying to get them out of the house.

Jerry Remy
September 28, 2012
Orioles at Red Sox
Top of the seventh, two out.
Jon Lester pitching to JJ Hardy.
Baltimore leading, 4-2

THE KINDNESS OF STRANGERS (WHAT WOULD YOU SAY?)
FOUND BY ERIC POULIN

Now—the kindness continues,
Here at Fenway.
Giving balls away to younger kids—
That's a nice thing.
Something Don probably would not do, but.........

If you think about it—
You know—
You've been waiting your whole life,
To maybe get a foul ball.
And all of a sudden you get one!
And there's this little kid that really, really wants one.

And Don would say:
No—it's mine.
I'm not going to play with it.
I'm gonna put it on my dashboard,
And listen to Dave Matthews.
On the way to the ballpark.

So, you can't have it.

Jerry Remy
September 25, 2014
Rays at Red Sox
Grant Balfour pitching to Yoenis Cespedes
Bottom of the 8th, one out.
Boston ahead, 11-1.

TRIUMPHS

BREAKING BARRIERS
FOUND BY MOLLY MCCLURE

It's a high fly
deep over centerfield

It is gone!

A black man
is getting a standing ovation
in the deep south
for breaking the record
of a baseball idol

It is over at ten minutes past nine
Hank Aaron has eclipsed the mark
set by
Babe Ruth

Vin Scully,
April 8, 1974
Dodgers at Braves
Bottom of the 4th, nobody out
Al Downing pitching to Henry Aaron
Los Angeles leading, 3-1

MOMENTS
FOUND BY MOLLY MCCLURE

What a marvelous moment
for baseball

what a marvelous moment
for Atlanta

what a marvelous moment
for the country and world

What a memorable moment
shaking hands with Dodgers on the infield

What a memorable moment
particularly for Hank Aaron

being met at home
by his parents

and all the Braves

Vin Scully
April 8, 1974
Dodgers at Braves
Al Downing pitching to Henry Aaron
Bottom of the 4th, nobody out
Los Angeles leading, 3-1

OH, DOCTOR
FOUND BY JAMES WALKER

Joe leans in.

Here's the pitch
swung on, *belted*
It's a long one, deep into left center.

Back goes Gionfriddo
back
back
back
back
back
back
he makes a one-handed catch against the bullpen.

Oh, doctor!

C
H
E
E
R
S

against the railing
in front of the bullpen
he reached up with one hand
and took a home run away from

DiMaggio.

Red Barber
October 5, 1947
Dodgers at Yankees
Joe Hatten pitching to Joe DiMaggio
Bottom of the sixth, two out
Dodgers leading, 8-5.

BELIEF...AND DISBELIEF-
MIKE BLOWSTRADAMUS
FOUND BY JORDAN NIELSEN

(i)

Well,
I think,
clearly
it's going to be Tuiasosopo today.

He's swung the bat well the last few times he's got an opportuni-
ty to play.
I expect him to hit
his first
big league
home run
today.

He's going to get a good count today.
He's going to get a fastball.
And he's going to hit it out of left center field.

Probably, oh, maybe…in the second deck
on a 3-1 count
it'll be a fastball, he's a fastball pitcher,
3-1 count
second at-bat
second deck.

Mike Blowers
September 27, 2009
Seattle at Toronto
Pregame Show

I've never been so excited about a 3-1 count in my life.

I don't believe it!
I see the light!
I believe you Mike!
Unbelievable!

I have never in my life
Seen
Such a prediction
Come true.

Dave Niehaus
September 27, 2009
Seattle at Toronto
Brian Tallet pitching to Matt Tuiasosopo
Top of the 5th, nobody out, nobody on.
Seattle leading, 1-0.

LONG GONE
FOUND BY DAN D'ADONNA

And ...

here's the pitch ...

He swings and there's a

LOOOOOONNNNGGG drive to right

And it's a HOME RUN for Gibson,

A three-run homer

and the Tigers lead it 8 to 4!

Ernie Harwell
October 14, 1984
Padres at Tigers
Goose Gossage pitching to
Kirk Gibson
Bottom of the eighth, two out
Detroit leading 5-4

HOW ABOUT THAT
FOUND BY ROBERT ZUSSMAN

Here's the pitch.

Mantle swings.

There's a tremendous drive

going into deep left field!

It's going, going!

It's over the bleachers...

over the sign atop the bleachers...

into the yards of houses across the street!

It's got to be one of the longest home runs I've ever seen!

How about that!

Mel Allen
April 17, 1953
Yankees at Senators
Chuck Stobbs pitching
to Mickey Mantle
Top of the fifth, two out
New York leading, 2-1

ALL THE WAY TO MARBLEHEAD
FOUND BY ERIC POULIN

i.

Three outs left, just three homers for McGwire
(The *most impressive* three).

Make it four!
Back back back back–
Gone!

ii.

OH back back back back—onto the Massachusetts Turnpike–

iii.

A little higher but *just as handsome*
Six home runs!

iv.

He's our leader! Hello Boston!

v.

This one's headed to the flagpole…
Salute the flag! Home run number eight!
And I'll tell you what—we weren't that far from a million bucks!

McGwire has 18 lifetime home runs in Fenway
For road parks he's only hit more in Tiger Stadium
The guy only has warning track power—what's wrong with him?

vi.

Hello, New Hampshire!

vii.

This one could be all the way.........to Maine!

viii.

Sends this one back back back back back—gone!

ix.

OHHHHH—I think they've got to build a wall–maybe eighty feet.
You think Tim Flannery has a job
Just in case Dave McKay gets a sore arm with the Cardinals?

x.

OHHH—back back back back—it's all the way to Marblehead!

In a single round, we've never seen 13 home runs before.
But then again, we've never seen 70 either.

Chris Berman
July 12, 1999
MLB All-Star Home Run Derby
Tim Flannery pitching to Mark McGwire

KILLING LAVAGETTO
FOUND BY JAMES WALKER

Gionfriddo walks off second
Miksis, off first
They're both ready to go on anything.

Two men out, last of the ninth.
The pitch, swung on.
There's a drive hit out toward the right field corner.
Henrich is going back, he can't get it

Here comes the tying run

Here comes the winning run.

C

H

E

E

R

I

N

G

Fans,

they're *killing Lavagetto*.

His own teammates!

They're beating him to pieces!

And it's taking a police escort to get *Lavagetto away* from the Dodgers.

Red Barber
October 3, 1947
Yankees at Dodgers
Bill Bevens pitching to
Cookie Lavagetto
Bottom of the 9th, two out (Game Four, 1947 World Series)
New York leading Brooklyn, 2-1

DALE SVEUM'S EASTER
SUNDAY HOME RUN
FOUND BY BOB RUSSON

---

three and two
two outs
four - four
ninth inning
Gantner - there he goes
a swing and a fly ball
right field and deep!
  get up
    get up
      get outa here
        gone!

Bob Uecker
April 19, 1987
Texas at Milwaukee
Greg Harris pitching to Dale Sveum
Bottom of the 9th, two out
Game tied, 4-4

SHOCKED TO HIS TOE
FOUND BY MARK SCHWABER

You know, I said it once before.

A few days ago.

That Kirk Gibson was not the most valuable player.
The most valuable player for the Dodgers was Tinkerbell.
But tonight I think Tinkerbell backed off for Kirk Gibson.

And look at Eckersley

Shocked to his toe.

Vin Scully
October 15, 1988
Athletics at Dodgers
Dennis Eckersley pitching to Kirk Gibson
Bottom of the 9th, two out
Oakland leading Los Angeles, 4-3.

OH MY GOD!
FOUND BY PALLAS GUTIERREZ

Oh my God!
Todo lo malo, échalo pa' allá.
April 4: Nobody in the ballpark. 0–5. Hitless through seven. Feels like rock bottom.

Oh my God!
Dame salud y prosperidad.

No tengo nada, pero soy feliz.
Solo recuerdos habitan en mí.

May 25: The Mets are now 9–22 in their last 31 games. Remember, the sun will come up tomorrow, as difficult as that may be to realize.

Sueños que cumplir
y yo voy a mí.
Puede que esté crazy, pero no lazy,
y hasta lograrlo, voy a seguir.

June 28: It is gone! A line drive home run over the right field wall for Jeff McNeil. The Mets have opened up a 6–2 lead over the Astros.

Oh my God!
Todo lo malo, échalo pa' allá.

September 30: Ground ball. Lindor waits on it. He's got it, and the ball game is over! From 0–5 to OMG, what a ride! The Mets are going to the postseason in 2024!

Oh my God!
Dame salud y prosperidad.

Gary Cohen, Wayne Randazzo, and Candelita (aka Jose Iglesias)
Various dates in 2024

AND THE RAYS ARE GOING TO ASK
FOUND BY BISHOP NAVARRO

for the biggest hit in the life of Brett Phillips. Traded
to Tampa Bay from Kansas City. Hit under
.200 with both organizations this year. Hit two home runs.
The 26-year-old outfielder. Now the question's gonna be
is will he think his best chance is on the first pitch.
Will he be aggressive? What a moment.
Not on the roster during the LCS, added for the World Series,
and here he is. Ball one inside from Jansen. Not one,
not too many people sitting down. Phillips, that caught
the corner. One ball, one strike. Born in Florida, trying to deliver
for Tampa Bay. Tying run at second, winning run at first. Two out
in the ninth. Outside corner, strike two. Real close. Phillips has
got to fight now, two strikes. Jansen.

That is into center field! Here comes Kiermaier,
Phillips has tied the game!
Arozarena coming around–
–throw home,
now he stumbles...
...But the ball gets away!
Tampa Bay wins it!

Brett Phillips,
Game 4,
hero.

Joe Buck
October 24, 2020
Dodgers at Rays
Kenley Jensen pitching to Brett Phillips
Bottom of the 9th, two out
Los Angeles leading, 7-6

CAN YOU BELIEVE IT?
FOUND BY JOANNE HULBERT

Swing and a ground ball
Stabbed by Foulke.
He has it,
He underhands to first —
And the Boston Red Sox
Are the world champions.
For the first time in 86 years
The Red Sox have won
Baseball's world championship.
Can you believe it?

Joe Castiglione
October 27, 2004
Red Sox at Cardinals
Keith Foulke pitching to Edgar Renteria
Bottom of the 9th, two out
Boston leading, 3-0

CALLED SHOT IN TORONTO
FOUND BY GABRIEL BOGART

Tuiasosopo steps up to the plate
a mild, mid-6os Toronto afternoon
Rick Rizzs along with Mike Blowers
for our Picks to Click, Mike…
…who's yours?

Well, I think, clearly
it's going to be Tuiasosopo today
he's swung the bat well
the last few times
he's gotten the opportunity to play…
…I expect him to hit
his first big-league home run today
he's gonna get in a good count today
he's gonna get a fastball from Tallet
and
he's going to hit it out to left-center
maybe in the second deck

Okay, alright
and I'm lookin' forward to it
Matt Tuiasosopo's first home run of his career
coming up, according to Mike Blowers

On a 3-1 count

On a 3-1 count?
Breaking ball? Fastball?

It'll be a fastball,
he's a fastball pitcher

Second deck?
How many rows back?

I, I can't thi-
'cuz people get their hands in the way
so you never know

And the left-hander's 2-1 pitch
and that's inside! ball three

I've never been so excited
on a 3-1 count in my life
How 'bout that?
let's see what happens here
it's gonna be a fastball, Matt
Niehaus: yeah, we do know that.

now, the left-hander's 3-1 pitch on the way

swung on and belted!!!

into left field!

second deck!

fly fly, fly away
I don't believe it!

I've seen the light

two-to-nothing Mariners,
he missed the second deck
by just, a little bit
and Matt Tuiasosopo
has made the prediction come true...

...I have never in my life
seen such a prediction come true

Mike Blowers, you are unbelievable
Matt Tuiasosopo, his first major-league home run
WOW.

Dave Niehaus, Mike Blowers, and Rick Rizzs
September 27, 2009
Mariners at Blue Jays
Brian Tallet pitching to Matt Tuiasosopo
Top of the 5 th, no out.
Mariners leading 1-0.

OUTDONE HIMSELF
FOUND BY PALLAS GUTIERREZ

2-1 to Lindor,
now the pitch.
Swing

and a drive

towards the gap in right-center.

It's pretty deep,

it's back

near the wall!

It's gone! It's gone! Francisco Lindor, he may have just outdone him-
self! He has hit a grand slam into the Phillies bullpen in right-center
field. The Mets were famished for the big hit all night, and Francisco
Lindor just provided a feast!

Mets four,
Phillies one
here in the sixth inning.

Howie Rose,
October 9, 2024.
Phillies at Mets
Carlos Estévez pitching to Francisco Lindor
Bottom of the sixth, bases loaded, 1 out
Philadelphia leading, 1-0

WHAT A STUDY
FOUND BY ERIC POULIN

What a study of a manager.

Darrell Johnson.

And what a study of fans.

And what a study of a bench.

There he is!
Bernie Carbo

Two base hits—
Two home runs!

Joe Garagiola
October 21, 1975
Reds at Red Sox—Game Six of the World Series
Rawley Eastwick pitching to Bernie Carbo
Bottom of the 8th, two out
Game tied, 6-6.

TRAGEDIES

BITTER PILL (A TRAGEDY FOR TWO VOICES)
FOUND BY KURT BLUMENAU

Davis three steps off first base now.

Bill goes to the plate:
Crawford swings,
A drive to right field,

That ball is going to ... be.... gone!

A home run!
The game is over!

Willie Crawford
With his fourth home run in as many games
And the whole Dodger team is going to be out to greet him
When he comes to home plate!

What a heartbreaking defeat for Bill Stoneman.
He was within one pitch of ending this game –
One strike –
Of sending it into extra innings, I should say,
And Crawford hits it out right down the right-field line.

An outstanding performance by Bill Stoneman
Spoiled by Willie Crawford with two outs
And he hit the 1-2 pitch down the right-field line
Into the seats,
A two-run homer,
And the Dodgers win it.

– – – –

Crawford's two-run homer
His fourth of the year
In as many games.
Davis scoring the run ahead of him.

Two runs, one hit
No errors, nobody left.
What can you say?

A bitter pill for Bill Stoneman and the Expos
To swallow here tonight.

When Bill saw that ball go out,
He just put his hands on his knees
And bowed down in the infield
And stared at the ground
While Crawford made the rounds.

The Dodgers win it
In the bottom of the ninth
With two outs
On Crawford's home run.

The final, Los Angeles 2, Montreal nothing,
And I'll have the totals in a minute.

Dave Van Horne and Russ Taylor
April 26, 1972
Montreal at Los Angeles
Bill Stoneman pitching to Willie Crawford
Bottom of the 9th, Two out, runner on first
Scoreless game

BEHIND THE BAG
FOUND BY ERIC POULIN

little

R
   O
      L
         L
           E
              R

Up.

Along first.

Behind the bag??????

it gets through Buckner

here.
comes.
Knight.

       and

                  the

   mets

             win

it..

Vin Scully
October 26, 1986
Red Sox at Mets
Bob Stanley pitching to Mookie Wilson
Bottom of the 10th, two out
Game tied at 5

I WISH
FOUND BY ERIC POULIN

I wish I could have had that kind of fun playing.
You know?
I really do.

I mean—
I could never,
I could never,
Never be comfortable.

You know if I had a good night,
I was almost thinking,
Well, the next night's going to turn around,
And be a bad night.

It was just the stress,
Of playing daily.
Every single day.

I just couldn't enjoy the game,
The way I wish I could have.

Jerry Remy
July 27, 2020
Mets at Red Sox
Zack Godley pitching to J.D. Davis
Top of the 7th, one out
New York leading, 7-2

WHAT THE 2024 METS WERE ALL ABOUT
FOUND BY PALLAS GUTIERREZ

It's certainly understandable,
if you are emotionally invested in this Mets team,
and you're sad right now.

September 30: Slowly hit to short, waiting on it Lindor. He's got it,
throws to first. Put it in the books! The New York Mets are headed
to postseason play in what has been a memorable season.

But I promise you,
if it ends here,
if they don't pull off some kind of magical comeback,
once the immediate disappointment wears off,
you'll realize what an incredible ride this team took you for this year.

October 3: Here's the pitch. Swing and a fly ball to right field. Pretty
well hit. It's gone! He did it! He did it! Pete Alonso keeps this fairy-
tale season going with the fairytale swing of his career.

Started out 0-5,
showed some signs of life,
before they fell to 11 games under the .500 mark,
and a lot of people had them written off right there.
Even if they don't pull the Houdini act of all time off,
somehow the Mets,
they're just not going quietly.

October 9: Swung on and missed, strike three! Put it in the books!
And to the New York Mets, California here we come! They have
defeated the Philadelphia Phillies 4-1.

When you're lying around during the offseason,
anticipating the next one,
and you think about what the 2024 Mets were all about,
you won't be able to keep yourself from smiling.
"Transitional year, they're punting on the season."
Well, they've kicked all the way
to the sixth game of the National League Championship Series.

October 21: Here's Alvarez. Bouncing ball to the right side, Taylor up
with it, throws to first, in time! And the Los Angeles Dodgers have
won the 2024 National League pennant.

You can watch baseball for a lot of years,
and never see the run that the Mets went on during this postseason.
It's poetic, isn't it?

Howie Rose
Various dates in 2024

ONE LAST TIME
FOUND BY ERIC POULIN

Well, it was an incredible moment to drive up
You realize you're driving up for the last time
You realize that everything you've done since you opened your eyes
this morning
Is probably going to be done
In this order and for this reason

For the last time

And when you pull up and you see the people
You see the reasons you have been able to get up in the morning
The reasons when you felt like you were behind the 8-ball

You were able to get motivated
To get that extra mile in
To do that extra set
Because you knew you had people
Who were spending their hard-earned money
And their time
And looking to create memories
And you were going to be a part of that

And so today

I just wanted to take the opportunity
To go out and be around the folks who are responsible
For this place having the heartbeat that it has had
For FIFTY-SEVEN years

An unparalleled level of energy
Pounding its way through the concrete

Day in and day out
Summer in and summer out

And even as the calendar has turned to fall
As the tears fall
We have one more opportunity today
To show each other
How much we love each other

To show this team how much we love them
And to just be fans of Oakland A's baseball

One last time.

Dallas Braden
September 26, 2024
Rangers at Athletics
Pregame Show

GOODBYE, FAREWELL, AND AMEN

YOU DESERVE IT, EARL
FOUND BY ERIC POULIN

You are bearing witness to one of the most remarkable scenes,
Maybe that you will ever see in sports.

Yes the fans have stayed—
They have stayed to cheer,
And to honor the retiring manager
of the birds of Baltimore.

A man who in fifteen years has become an absolute legend.

The defeat will *hurt*.

There's Harvey Kuenn over to congratulate him—
And Earl Weaver is crying.

And you can understand it

Very rarely has there been a scene like this.

If ever.

These people of this city,
A city that has become a beautiful city,
Under a brilliant Mayor.
With an inner harbor *equivalent of Boston???????*

And that's Edgar Bennett Williams.
The owner—the great criminal attorney.

And there they are standing and chanting.
ALL of them in unison

And the sign says it all, Earl.

And you deserve it.

One of the greatest managers
In the history of the game.

Howard Cosell
October 3, 1982
Brewers at Orioles
Post-game analysis
Milwaukee won, 10-2

ALMOST A HAIKU
FOUND BY ERIC POULIN

Gonna stretch right now.
Gotta reduce some endorphins.
I am stressed right now.

Jerry Remy (Final call of career)
July 28, 2021
Blue Jays at Red Sox (Doubleheader Game Two)
Matt Barnes pitching to Santiago Espinal.
Top of the seventh, one out.
Boston leading, 4-1.

HUB FANS BICK MICK SALUT
FOUND BY MARK STERNMAN

And let's see the reaction to Mantle's appearance....
Standing ovation!
Not everybody up,
but of around 30,000 in the ballpark,
I'd say 15, 18, perhaps 20,000 up on their feet.
And now as you look to the outfield,
they're all up.

Frank Messer
September 27, 1968
Yankees at Red Sox
Dick Ellsworth pitching to Mickey Mantle
Top of the first, one out, one on.
Scoreless game

MEANING MAKERS
FOUND BY BYRON PETRAROJA

To the Dodgers in seventh place and the .45's in ninth, the game
meant someth'n.
To the 6,000 plus, who attended on a drizzly, cloudy, humid day, the
game meant someth'n .
And with 20-win seasons, team records, and old scores to be settled,
the game meant
someth'n.
For in any story, show, or sporting event, there exists a defining
moment that rises and hovers
above the rest, bringing meaning to all.
And such was the task for Elston and Passe,
to paint on a palette not seen on a screen or witnessed in person.
It happened during inning nine with the teams locked in time
and space.
No runs had been scored, neither team wanting to yield.
With Tommy Davis on second and Johnny Roseboro at the plate
Gene Elston made the call that brought meaning to all.
He described the path of the ball that caused Joe Morgan to fall
and then scamper to his feet in a manner so fleet
that he was able to spot Davis bearing down on Grote guarding
his plate.
Then Elston, in his trademark economical style, holding his excite-
ment for this specific moment
in time —- made the call,
"… Here comes Tommy Davis in to score, the play at the plate is —-
in time. They got
him!"
Then he paused to allow us to hear the 6,000 plus roar, for now the
game did matter to all.
Satisfied that the moment had exhaled, he delivered a recap for his
audience to savor,

"Tommy Davis is struck down at the plate by Joe Morgan to Grote
on a play that will not
ever be any closer than that one."
And so, even though no consequence did it bore on the pennant race
of '64, the game truly
meant someth'n.

Gene Elston
September 27, 1964
Dodgers at Colt .45's
Bob Bruce pitching to John Roseboro
Top of the 9th, 2 out
Scoreless game

ON A NAPKIN
FOUND BY ERIC POULIN

I'm going to ask you to do something for me right now—

You know that the first autograph I ever received
Was a Dave Stewart autograph.
And it was an autograph
On a Taco Bell napkin
That my mother had got during one of the signings
That you had done in the city.

And after a move
I was not able to find that napkin anymore.

But I do have a napkin here with me today
And I have an opportunity to maybe get your autograph on a ball.

But Stew—that's not going to do it for me.

If you would be so kind
I would love to have your autograph on a napkin
And this means more to me than any baseball you could ever sign.

Dallas Braden (speaking to Dave Stewart)
September 22, 2024
Yankees at Athletics
Luis Gil pitching to Lawrence Butler
Bottom of the 2nd, 2 out
Game tied, 2-2

A TOUGH DAY FOR EVERYBODY

FOUND BY ERIC POULIN

Hey, you know—

We're going to be paying tributes all day long to you
And I know you're going to address the fans
Later on in the ballgame
But I'd like to take a moment to say something now
That the last fifteen years has been an absolute pleasure
Working with you.

And you know we've grown a lot together
We've gone through a lot together
And I value your professionalism in the job
And also the fact that we've very good friends
And I'm going to miss that tremendously.

And I want to thank you for all the fun moments we've had.

And your friendship.

And today's a tough day for everybody.

Jerry Remy (to Don Orsillo)
October 4, 2015
Red Sox at Indians
Rick Porcello pitching to Roberto Perez
Bottom of the 4th, nobody out
Cleveland leading, 3-1.

STING
FOUND BY ERIC POULIN

And The Crew

Will—um...

Will have it end,

Here tonight................

I'm telling ya—

That one?

Had some sting on it....

Bob Uecker (Final call of career)
October 3, 2024
Mets at Brewers
Post-game show
Mets won, 4-2

ALL THESE YEARS
FOUND BY ERIC POULIN

And speaking of fan appreciation
As a fan
And believe me—I'll always be a fan
Let me express my appreciation to the Cubs organization.

For all these years.

And to WGN and the Chicago Tribune organization.

All these years.

And all the people associated with both organizations
For the privilege of being on this scene.

I intend to stay on the scene for a while
I'm moving away from play by play.

After all these years.

But—I'm going to be around
And I hope we'll meet somewhere along the line.

In the meantime again—let me say—as one fan to another
I appreciate you
And I really appreciate too—the kindness that you've shown me.

I'm Jack Brickhouse—that's it from Wrigley Field
For now.............

CODA

(Stay tuned for American League action
as our White Sox take on the Oakland A's next.)

Jack Brickhouse (final call of career)
September 27, 1981
Philadelphia at Chicago
Post-game show
Phillies won, 14-0

CONTRIBUTORS

JIM ARMENTI is a musician, teacher and poet living in western Massachusetts, where he lives with his wife, dog and cat. Two grown children and a daughter-in-law visit often enough, and good neighbors are always around. His main work is with the Lonesome Brothers Band, the Young at Heart Chorus, Klezamir and the Klines, and he teaches music at Downtown Sounds Workers Cooperative in Northampton. He is an avid (season's tickets with the Valley Blue Sox) baseball, football, basketball and hockey fan, and loves this project as an intersection of many threads in the Pioneer Valley.

GABRIEL BOGART is from Seattle, Washington. Gabe is a lifelong Supersonics fan and impatiently awaits their return. He has written poetry, short stories, creative non-fiction, music reviews, interviews, and marketing blurbs. When not writing, he is busy with synthesizers and drum machines, listening to records, watching baseball, basketball, and movies, painting, reading, and cooking. Ice cream is a Kryptonite-level weakness for Gabe.

KURT BLUMENAU grew up in the Rochester, New York, area, following the Mets and the Triple-A Rochester Red Wings. He works in corporate communications in the Boston area. He has a strong interest in the minor leagues, particularly the New York-Penn League, and also enjoys watching college games.

FRANK CRESSOTTI began teaching studio art and introduction to art at Holyoke (MA) Community College in 1969. During his over 40-year career of teaching, he was the longtime Chair of the Art Department and was Curator of the Taber Art Gallery at HCC until 2024. He holds a BA from Gettysburg College in Pennsylvania and an MFA in Painting from Ohio University.

DAN D'ADONNA is the sports editor at *The Holland Sentinel* and Northern Sports Team Leader for the USA TODAY Network Center for Community Journalism. He is involved in the Society for American Baseball Research (SABR) and has written two books: *In Cobb's Shadow: The Hall of Fame Careers of Sam Crawford, Harry Heilmann and Heinie Manush* and *Golden Glow*, a biography of Olympic gold medal swimmer Kaitlin Sandeno.

T. S. FLYNN is an educator and writer based in Minneapolis. He's a member of the Halsey Hall Chapter of the Society for American Baseball Research (SABR).

HARRISON GOLDEN is a retired Little League first baseman who found his second act in journalism. He has served as a news reporter, photographer, anchor, and producer. His work has appeared on the platforms of NBC News, Fox News, CNN, *Interview, Reader's Digest*, and *USA Today*. He is a contributing writer and fact-checker for SABR's Games Project. Born and raised in New York, he currently lives in North Carolina.

PALLAS GUTIERREZ is a writer, fiber artist, and passionate Mets fan. They are pursuing their MFA in Creative Writing through the University of California, Riverside, and waiting not so patiently for Opening Day. Pallas is working on a bildungsroman novel about a road trip to every ballpark. They review books and share their writing on their Instagram account @sunandsealibrary.

JOANNE HULBERT is a Boston Chapter member and SABR Baseball and the Arts Committee cochair, who knows well that although baseball is designed to break your heart, there are moments of great joy that remind us all that waiting for next year will be worth it.

MOLLY MCCLURE was born and raised in West Hartford, CT. She grew up a divided household between the cathedral in the Bronx and Fenway. Today she is a preschool teacher in New London New Hampshire. In her spare time she loves to go out with her son Ian and husband Bruce exploring Vermont and New Hampshire. She also cares for her beloved cat Gus.

JORDAN NIELSEN is a native of the Pacific Northwest where he grew to love baseball watching Ken Griffey Jr., Randy Johnson, Edgar Martinez, and others in the prime of their careers. He works as an organizational psychologist and professor at Purdue University in West Lafayette, IN, where he teaches, conducts research, and consults to organizations about employee well-being and purpose in the workplace. Among other topics, he is currently researching how businesses can learn lessons from major league umpires about decision-making and navigating changes to one's professional identity.

RAY L. NIELSEN of Aloha, Oregon, is a recently retired Financial/Budget Analyst in state and local government. A former high school jock and sports lover, Ray is a poet, storyteller, Seattle Mariners fan, husband, father of five sons and grandfather of sixteen grandchildren.

BYRON PETRAROJA is a retired Syracuse city public school teacher and a current SABR member. During the early stages of his teaching career, he was introduced to the field of storytelling and has since told stories in the classroom and at various community settings including The National Baseball Hall of Fame in Cooperstown, NY. This is his initial attempt at submitting a poetic piece for SABR and has thoroughly enjoyed the process.

ERIC POULIN is a Professor of Library and Information Science at Simmons University, where he directs their western Massachusetts-based satellite campus in Greenfield, MA. Among many weird quirks, he is known as being an authority on the history of baseball in Holyoke, Massachusetts—particularly the old Holyoke Millers of the Eastern League. He believes with all his heart that John Fisher should sell the Athletics in order for the team to return to the City of Oakland where they belong.

MARK SCHWABER is a New England-based singer, songwriter, and guitarist who has recorded with Lloyd Cole, Matthew Sweet, Mary Lou Lord, Shadows Fall, Joel Stroetzel of Killswitch Engage, and has performed live with Glen Hansert. He has also released over ten albums eponymously, as well as with the bands Home and Hospital.

HART SEELY is the editor of several collections of "found" poetry, including verses by Phil Rizzuto and Donald Rumsfeld. He is also publisher of AHOY Comics.

The game that **MARK S. STERNMAN** listened to for this book took place on the day of his birth and featured the Yankees, his favorite team, and the Red Sox, his least favorite (although he loves Fenway Park and has held a partial season ticket plan for the Sox since the terrible 2004 season). Sternman believes that Ogden Nash's "Line-Up for Yesterday: An ABC of Baseball Immortals" remains the best baseball poem of all time.

CECILIA TAN has been SABR's Publications Director since 2011 and has overseen the publication of over 100 books in her SABR tenure. Her sporadically updated baseball blog can be found at WhyILikeBaseball.com.

DR. JAMES R. WALKER is an Emeritus Professor of Communication at Saint Xavier University and past Executive Director of the International Association for Communication and Sport. Walker has written about baseball and the electronic media for four decades, authoring six books and dozens of scholarly articles. His most recent books are *Center Field Shot: A History of Baseball on Television* (with Robert V. Bellamy), *Crack of the Bat: A History of Baseball on the Radio*, and *Red Barber: The Life and Legacy of a Broadcasting Legend* (with Judith R. Hiltner), all published by the University of Nebraska Press. Walker enjoys playing fantasy baseball (with considerable success he might, and does, add).

TIM WILES is a retired librarian who lives in Guilderland, NY. From 1995-2014, he directed the A. Bartlett Giamatti Research Center, within the National Baseball Hall of Fame Library in Cooperstown. He is the co-editor of *Line Drives: 100 Contemporary Baseball Poems* (Southern Illinois University Press, 2002), and the co-author of *Baseball's Greatest Hit: The Story of Take Me Out to the Ball Game* (Hal Leonard, 2008). His article on baseball poetry, "Who's On Verse" ran in the Sunday *New York Times* on Opening Day in 1996. He is widely known for his costumed performances of "Casey At the Bat."

DR. ROBERT ZUSSMAN was a Professor Emeritus in the Sociology Department at the University of Massachusetts at Amherst. He was the author of *Intensive Care: Medical Ethics and the Medical Profession* and *Mechanics of the Middle Class: Work and Politics among American Engineers*. He was a lifelong New York Yankees fan, and his final publication before his untimely passing was *YANKALYTICS: An analytic history of the New York Yankees Baseball Team* (yankalytics.com).

www.ingramcontent.com/pod-product-compliance
Lightning Source LLC
Chambersburg PA
CBHW020419130626
46549CB00006B/2635